The Age of Dinosaurs

Meet Velociraptor

Written by Jayne Raymond

Illustrations by Leonello Calvetti and Luca Massini

Cavendish Square

New York

Published in 2015 by Cavendish Square Publishing, LLC
243 5th Avenue, Suite 136, New York, NY 10016

Library of Congress Cataloging-in-Publication Data

Raymond, Jayne, author.
Meet Velociraptor / Jayne Raymond.
pages cm. — (The age of dinosaurs)
Includes index.
ISBN 978-1-62712-779-0 (hardcover) ISBN 978-1-62712-780-6 (paperback) ISBN 978-1-62712-781-3 (ebook)
1. Velociraptor—Juvenile literature. 2. Dinosaurs—Juvenile literature. I. Title.

QE862.S3R383 2015
567.912—dc23

2014006642

Editorial Director: Dean Miller
Copy Editor: Cynthia Roby
Art Director: Jeffrey Talbot
Designer: Douglas Brooks
Photo Researcher: J8 Media
Production Manager: Jennifer Ryder-Talbot
Production Editor: David McNamara
Illustrations by Leonello Calvetti and Luca Massini

The photographs in this book are used by permission and through the courtesy of: ekina/Shutterstock.com, 8; © iStockphoto.com/skif, 8; J. Lekavicius/Shutterstock.com, 8; hecke61/Shutterstock.com, 8; Kabacchi/file:Velociraptor mount.jpg/Wikimedia Commons, 20; Procy/Shutterstock.com, 21.

Printed in the United States of America

CONTENTS

Late Triassic	Early Jurassic	Middle Jurassic
227 – 206 million years ago.	206 –176 million years ago.	176 – 159 million years ago.

A CHANGING WORLD

One of the Earth's most intriguing creatures—the dinosaur—roamed a planet very different from the one we live in today: the continents were different, the climate was warmer, and grass did not exist yet.

The word "dinosaur" is originally from the Greek words *deinos* and *sauros*. Together, they mean "fearfully great lizards."

The lifetime of the Earth is broken down into geological time: eras, periods, epochs, and ages. Dinosaurs existed during the geological time period called the Mesozoic era. The Mesozoic era is divided into the Triassic period, which lasted 42 million years; the Jurassic

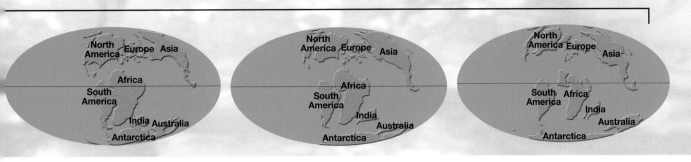

Late Jurassic	Early Cretaceous	Late Cretaceous
159 – 144 million years ago.	144 – 99 million years ago.	99 – 65 million years ago.

period, which lasted 61 million years; and the Cretaceous period, which lasted for 79 million years.

Dinosaurs became extinct almost 65 million years before the first humans appeared on Earth. None of your ancestors ever saw a living dinosaur—no matter how far back in time you trace your family tree.

A SPEEDY PREDATOR

Velociraptor (pronounced ve-LAH-se-RAP-ter) roamed Earth about 75 million years ago toward the end of the Cretaceous period. It lived in the dry semi-desert areas of central Asia. A member of the *Dromaeosauridae* family, the feathered, carnivorous (meat-eating) Velociraptor belongs to the order *Saurischia* and the suborder *Theropoda*. This order of dinosaurs lived between the late Triassic and the end of the Cretaceous period, from 225 to 65.5 million years ago. Saurischian dinosaurs are the ancestors of birds. Theropod dinosaurs are "beast-footed" bipeds—meaning two-footed—that never became extinct. Today they are known as birds.

The name Velociraptor is a combination of the Latin words *velox*, meaning swift, and *raptor*, meaning a robber. Velociraptor is also called the "speedy thief" because most of its food was gathered by stealing the eggs of other dinosaurs. It then used its swift long legs to make a quick getaway.

As an adult, Velociraptor's body measured up to 6.8 feet (2 meters) long and 1.6 feet (0.5 m) tall at the hip. It weighed up to 33 pounds (15 kilograms). The dinosaur could run up to 40 miles (64 kilometers) per hour, but only for a short time. This speed gave Velociraptor an advantage when fleeing predators.

FINDING VELOCIRAPTOR

Velociraptor lived about 75 million years ago in what today are the hot, sandy dunes of Central Asia's Mongolian Desert. Because many Velociraptor remains were found in one location, paleontologists believe that the dinosaurs roamed in packs.

Seventy-five million years ago however, Mongolia was not a desert. It was a savannah habitat—meaning tropical or subtropical grassland with trees scattered about. Velociraptor shared the habitat with a variety of other Dromaeosaurids, Troodontids, Alvarezsaurids, and Oviraptorids.

Central Asia

The Gobi Desert

Djadochta Formation, Mongolia

Barun Goyot Formation, Mongolia

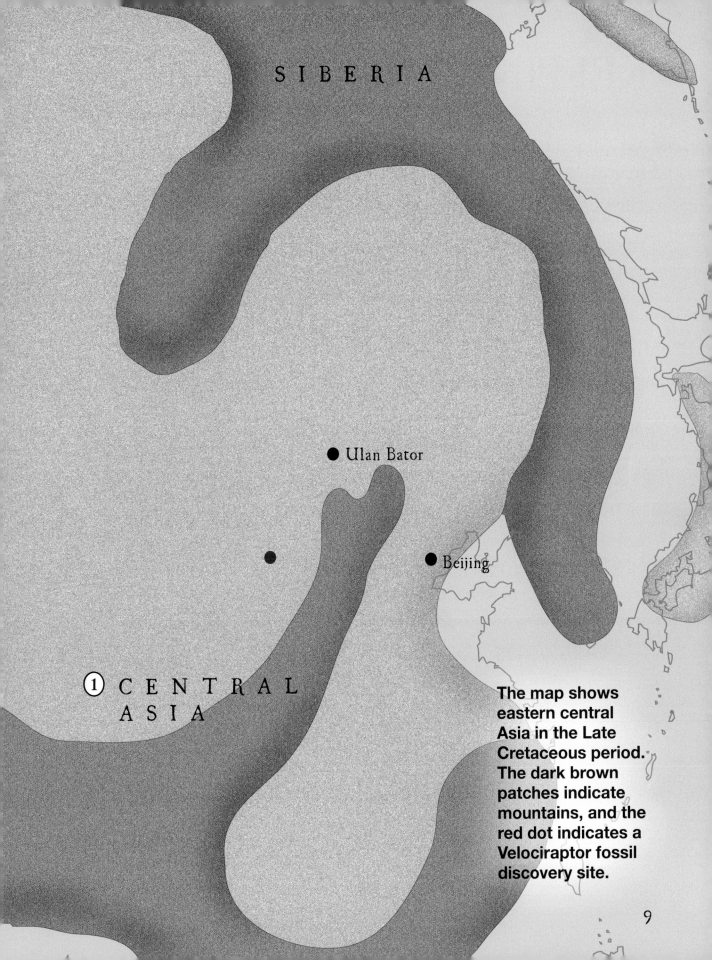

S I B E R I A

● Ulan Bator

●

① C E N T R A L
A S I A

● Beijing

The map shows
eastern central
Asia in the Late
Cretaceous period.
The dark brown
patches indicate
mountains, and the
red dot indicates a
Velociraptor fossil
discovery site.

KEEPING THE EGGS SAFE

Velociraptor's body was covered in small feathers, although it did not fly. The female used her feathers to protect her eggs, which measured from 3–6 inches (7.5–15 centimeters) in length. The number of eggs Velociraptor laid is unknown.

Velociraptor had to carefully choose the place to build its nest and lay its eggs—it had to be in the shade. Because the hot sun was dangerous for the eggs, Velociraptor used its body to shelter them from the heat, rainstorms, and from small primitive mammals in search of food.

YOUNG HUNTERS

Young Velociraptors were too small to hunt the larger dinosaurs that roamed near their habitat. Instead Velociraptor hunted smaller prey, such as small mammals and reptiles. The dinosaurs were also scavengers, eating leftover carcasses killed by larger dinosaurs.

Velociraptor jaws held 26 to 28 widely spaced teeth on each side—some measured over an inch (2.5 cm) long. The dinosaur would use its front claws to capture and hold the prey while it ate.

WARM OR COLD?

At one time, all dinosaurs were thought to be cold-blooded animals—meaning their body temperatures were close to the temperature of their environment. Although this is difficult to prove, paleontologists feel that Velociraptor was most likely a warm-blooded dinosaur—meaning that its blood remained warm and its body temperature did not change when the temperature of the environment changed.

Paleontologists suggest this theory because Velociraptor's body, like that of a bird, was covered with feathers—which would hold in the body's heat. Also, the dinosaur was aggressive when attacking its prey. It is uncommon for cold-blooded animals to exhibit this behavior.

FIGHTING DINOSAURS

The fossilized skeletons of a Velociraptor and a Protoceratops were unearthed from a red sandstone mound in Inner Mongolia, China, in 2008. The skeletons were found close together. Adult Velociraptor bite marks were found around the Protoceratops' jawbones. These findings caused paleontologists to first believe that the two dinosaurs died in mortal combat. However, research reveals that Velociraptor was only scavenging—or eating the flesh of—Protoceratops.

INSIDE VELOCIRAPTOR

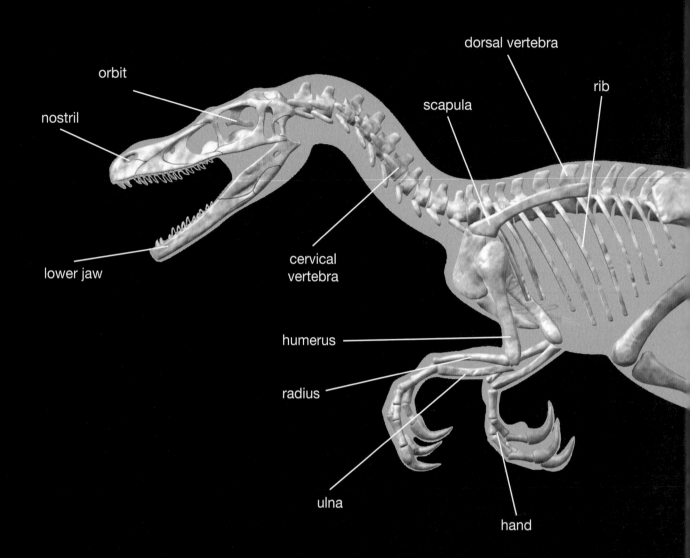

orbit

nostril

lower jaw

dorsal vertebra

scapula

rib

cervical
vertebra

humerus

radius

ulna

hand

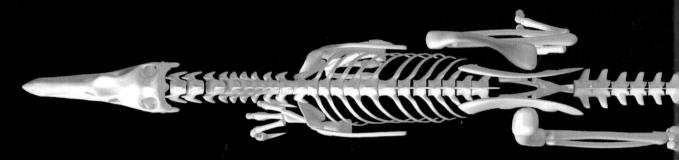

Dorsal view of skeleton

Velociraptor's egg-shaped head measured about 9 inches (23 cm) long with a noticeable upturned snout. The dinosaur used its sharp, 4-inch (10-cm) claws to tear away at its prey. They were also used to keep the prey from escaping. Its tail, made of hard fused bones, could not bend easily and balanced the dinosaur when making fast turns. Paleontologists believe that Velociraptor was able to jump as high as 10 feet (3 m) straight into the air.

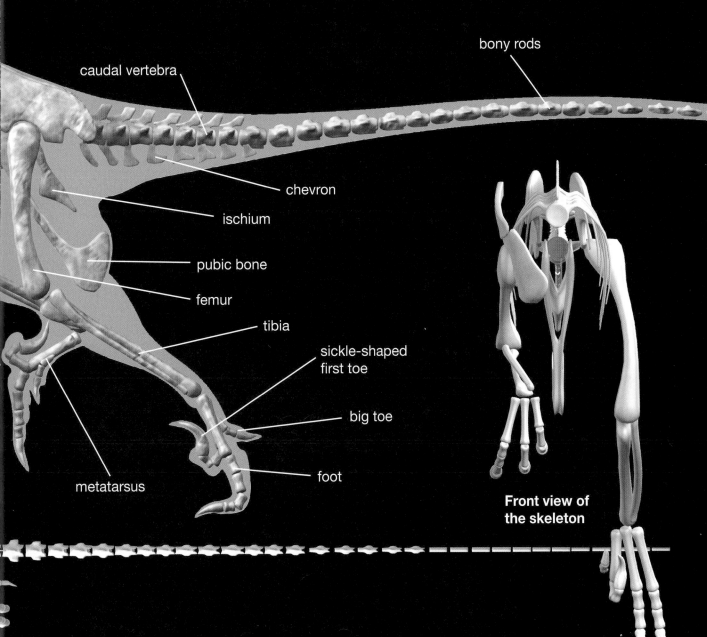

bony rods

caudal vertebra

chevron

ischium

pubic bone

femur

tibia

sickle-shaped first toe

big toe

foot

metatarsus

Front view of the skeleton

UNEARTHING VELOCIRAPTOR

In August of 1923, Peter Kaison set out on an expedition to the Outer Mongolian Gobi Desert. It was there that the paleontologist unearthed the first Velociraptor fossil. The skeleton had been damaged over time.

In the late 1980s, a joint Chinese and Canadian team unearthed Velociraptor fossils in northern China. More were found at the Flaming Cliffs site by a Mongolian and American team.

The forearm of a Velociraptor was discovered in 2007. It had the imprints of quills—meaning that there was finally proof that Velociraptor's body was covered in feathers and not reptilian scales.

To date, more than a dozen Velociraptor fossils have been uncovered. They consist of partial but connected skeletons and skulls, both of adult and young dinosaurs. This makes Velociraptor the best-known dromaeosaurid.

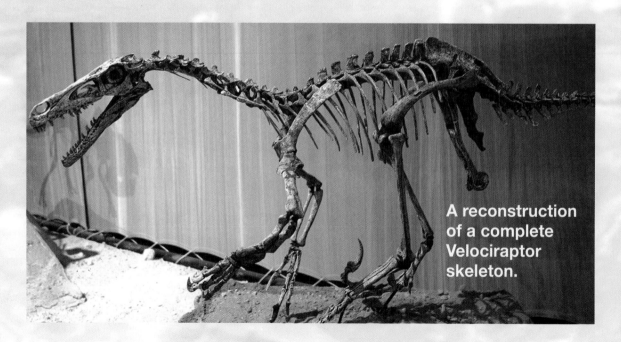

A reconstruction of a complete Velociraptor skeleton.

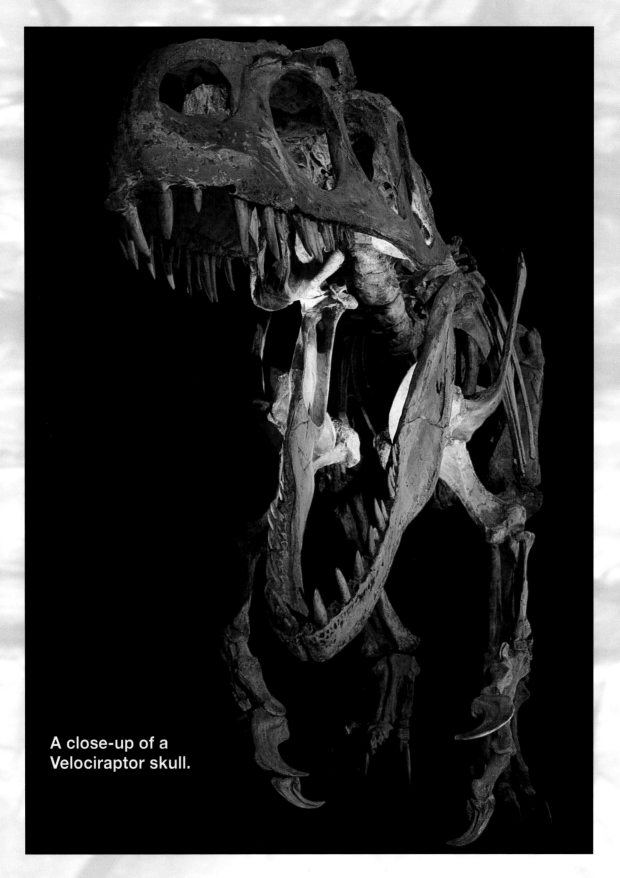

A close-up of a
Velociraptor skull.

THE FAMILY OF DEINONYCHOSAURIANS

Discovery sites of the Deinonychosaurians shown on these pages.

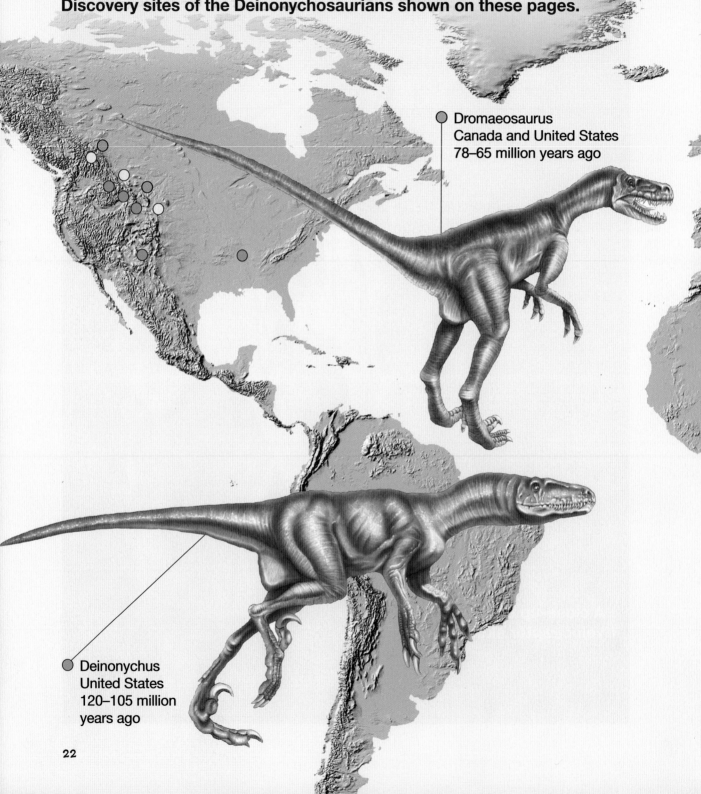

Dromaeosaurus
Canada and United States
78–65 million years ago

Deinonychus
United States
120–105 million
years ago

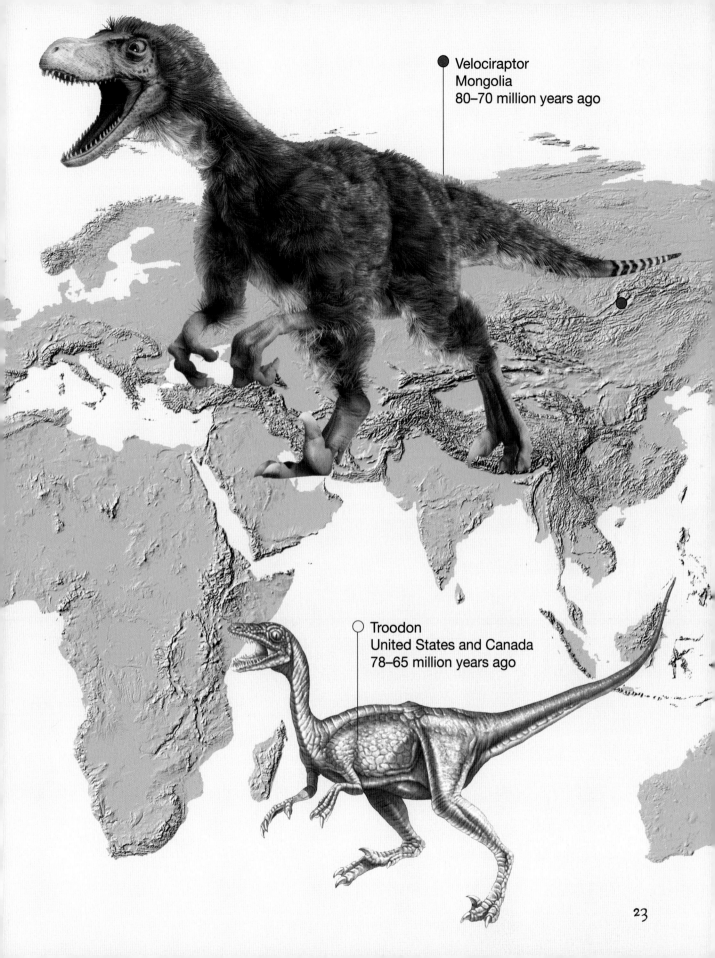

Velociraptor
Mongolia
80–70 million years ago

Troodon
United States and Canada
78–65 million years ago

THE GREAT EXTINCTION

Dinosaurs went extinct sixty-five million years ago. Many scientists think the impact of a huge meteorite from space may be to blame. They have found a crater caused by just such a meteorite off the Yucatan Peninsula in Mexico. The crater is 112 miles (180 kilometers) wide and nearly 3,000 feet (900 meters) deep.

While the meteor may have killed many dinosaurs on impact, many more would have died as a result of the cloud of dust that it must have kicked up. This cloud would have surrounded the earth, blocking out the sun and killing many plants. Food would have been scarce, and both plant- and meat-eating dinosaurs alike would have starved or frozen. However, some scientists think some dinosaurs may have survived this event and that present-day chickens and other birds may be descended from these dinosaurs.

A DINOSAUR'S FAMILY TREE

The oldest dinosaur fossils are 220–225 million years old and have been found all over the world.

Dinosaurs are divided into two groups. Saurischians are similar to reptiles, with the pubic bone directed forward, while the Ornithischians are like birds, with the pubic bone directed backward.

Saurischians are subdivided in two main groups: Sauropodomorphs, to which quadrupeds and vegetarians belong; and Theropods, which include bipeds and predators.

Ornithischians are subdivided into three large groups: Thyreophorans, which include the quadrupeds Stegosaurians and Ankylosaurians; Ornithopods; and Marginocephalians, which are subdivided into the bipedal Pachycephalosaurians and the mainly quadrupedal Ceratopsians.

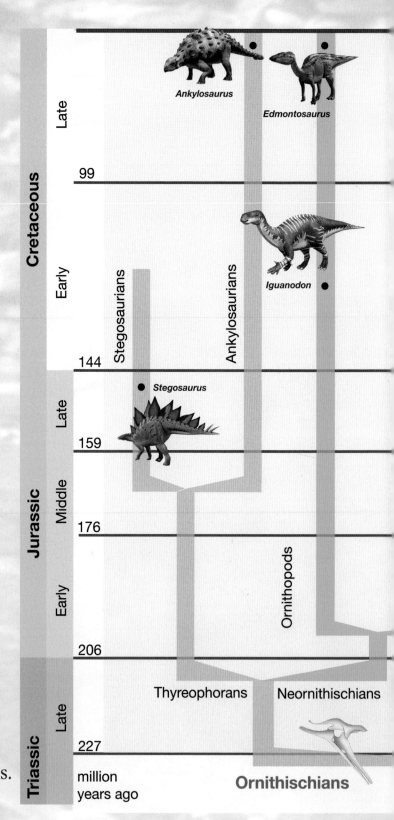

Cretaceous — Late — 99 — Early — 144

Jurassic — Late — 159 — Middle — 176 — Early — 206

Triassic — Late — 227

million years ago

Ankylosaurus
Edmontosaurus
Iguanodon
Stegosaurus

Stegosaurians

Ankylosaurians

Ornithopods

Thyreophorans

Neornithischians

Ornithischians

Triceratops

Pachycephalosaurus

Ornithomimus

Tyrannosaurus

Velociraptor

Giganotosaurus

Pachycephalosaurians

Ceratopsians

Ornithomimids

Tyrannosauroids

Oviraptorosaurians

Deinonychosaurians

Birds

Scipionyx

Deinonychus

Sauropods

Caudipteryx

Ornitholeste

Brachiosaurus

Diplodocus

Marginocephalians

Theropods

Prosauropods

Plateosaurus

Sauropodomorphs

Saurischians

Dinosauria

A SHORT VOCABULARY OF DINOSAURS

Bipedal: pertaining to an animal moving on two feet alone, almost always those of the hind legs.

Bone: hard tissue made mainly of calcium phosphate; single element of the skeleton.

Carnivore: a meat-eating animal.

Caudal: pertaining to the tail.

Cenozoic Era (Caenozoic, Tertiary Era): the interval of geological time between 65 million years ago and present day.

Cervical: pertaining to the neck.

Claws: the fingers and toes of predator animals end with pointed and sharp nails, called claws. Those of plant-eaters end with blunt nails, called hooves.

Cretaceous Period: the interval of geological time between 144 and 65 million years ago.

Egg: a large cell enclosed in a porous shell produced by reptiles and birds to reproduce themselves.

Epoch: a memorable date or event.

Evolution: changes in the character states of organisms, species, and higher ranks through time.

Extinct: when something, such as a species of animal, is no longer existing.

Feathers: outgrowth of the skin of birds and some dinosaurs, used in flight and in providing insulation and protection for the body. They evolved from reptilian scales.

Forage: to wander in search of food.

Fossil: evidence of life in the past. Not only bones, but footprints and trails made by animals, as well as dung, eggs, or plant resin, when fossilized, are fossils.

Herbivore: a plant-eating animal.

Jurassic Period: the interval of geological time between 206 and 144 million years ago.

Mesozoic Era (Mesozoic, Secondary Era): the interval of geological time between 248 and 65 million years ago.

Pack: a group of predator animals acting together to capture their prey.

Paleontologist: a scientist who studies and reconstructs the prehistoric life.

Paleozoic Era (Paleozoic, Primary Era): the interval of geological time between 570 and 248 million years ago.

Predator: an animal that preys on other animals for food.

Raptor (raptorial): a bird of prey, such as an eagle, hawk, falcon, or owl.

Rectrix (plural rectrices): any of the larger feathers in a bird's tail that are important in helping its flight direction.

Scavenger: an animal that eats dead animals.

Skeleton: a structure of an animal's body made of several different bones. One primary function is to protect delicate organs such as the brain, lungs, and heart.

Skin: the external, thin layer of the animal body. Skin cannot fossilize, unless it is covered by scales, feathers, or fur.

Skull: bones that protect the brain and the face.

Teeth: tough structures in the jaws used to hold, cut, and sometimes process food.

Terrestrial: living on land.

Triassic Period: the interval of geological time between 248 and 206 million years ago.

Unearth: to find something that was buried beneath the earth.

Vertebrae: the single bones of the backbone; they protect the spinal cord.

DINOSAUR WEBSITES

Dino Database
www.dinodatabase.com
Get the latest news on dinosaur research and discoveries.
This site is pretty advanced, so you may need help from a teacher
or parent to find what you're looking for.

Dinosaurs for Kids
www.kidsdinos.com
There's basic information about most dinosaur types, and you can
play dinosaur games, vote for your favorite dinosaur, and learn
about the study of dinosaurs, paleontology.

Dinosaur Train
pbskids.org/dinosaurtrain
From the PBS show *Dinosaur Train*, you can watch videos,
print out pages to color, play games, and learn lots of facts about
so many dinosaurs!

Discovery Channel Dinosaur Videos
discovery.com/video-topics/other/other-topics-dinosaur-videos.htm
Watch almost 100 videos about the life of dinosaurs!

The Natural History Museum
www.nhm.ac.uk/kids-only/dinosaurs
Take a quiz to see how much you know about dinosaurs—or a quiz
to tell you what type of dinosaur you'd be! There's also
a fun directory of dinosaurs, including some cool 3-D views of
your favorites.

MUSEUMS

American Museum of Natural History, New York, NY
www.amnh.org

Carnegie Museum of Natural History, Pittsburgh, PA
www.carnegiemnh.org

Denver Museum of Nature and Science, Denver, CO
www.dmns.org

Dinosaur National Monument, Dinosaur, CO
www.nps.gov/dino

The Field Museum, Chicago, IL
fieldmuseum.org

University of California Museum of Paleontology, Berkeley, CA
www.ucmp.berkeley.edu

Museum of the Rockies, Bozeman, MT
www.museumoftherockies.org

National Museum of Natural History, Smithsonian Institution,
Washington, DC
www.mnh.si.edu

Royal Tyrrell Museum of Palaeontology, Drumheller, Canada
www.tyrrellmuseum.com

Sam Noble Museum of Natural History, Norman, OK
www.snomnh.ou.edu

Yale Peabody Museum of Natural History, New Haven, CT
peabody.yale.edu

INDEX

Page numbers in **boldface** are illustrations.